Horia Ion Groza

The Sign of the North

Horia Ion Groza

The Sign of the North

Reflection Books
Sacramento, 2020

Title: The Sign of the North
Author: Horia Ion Groza
Photos on the front cover: Bryan Bowen
Painting on back cover: Bogdan Zaharescu
Three Drawings: Bogdan Zaharescu
Editor: Ioana L. Onica

ISBN: 978-1-936629-55-8

COPYRIGHT 2020 © REFLECTION BOOKS

Reflection Books, P.O. Box 1413
Citrus Heights, California 95611-1413
E-mail: info@reflectionbooks.com
www.reflectionbooks.com

For my friends and colleagues in Wisconsin

and for all my present and future friends

"Among man's faculties, the only one fundamental to his very being is his word. Poetry is a semantic tension toward the word not spoken yet. Poetry is all which differentiates man from all else"

Nichita Stănescu (Breaths)

Roses are red, violets are blue, poems are hard, potato.

Contents

Preface 13
Northwoods Songs 15
   Potato 17
   Hot Summer Dry Day 18
   Bryan's Dawn 22
   The Two White Ducks 24
   Planting at the Experimental Station 29
   Harvest 31
   First Day 33
   Tennis 37
   Hodag's Purgatory 39
   My Love Is Far 43
   Deer Day 44
   Winter in Northwoods 47
   Birds and Seasons 49
Father – Son Poems 51
   Lullaby 53
   My Little Son and the Geometry 54
   The Impossible 55
   Domestic Epic 56
   Silent Watch 57
   Water Is Soft 58
Life of the Poems 59
   Every Story 61
   The Birth of the Word 62
   My Poem 65
   Of Course 66

The Poem Punctuation 67
　　Spring Day 69
　　The Poem's Fate 70
　　The Song of Heart 71

Thy Love, O Lord 73
　　Psalm 1 75
　　Psalm 2 76
　　Psalm 3 77
　　Psalm 4 78
　　Psalm 5 80
　　Psalm 6 81
　　Thorns of Intrusion 83
　　Autumn Dusk 84
　　Anxious Hour 86

Poems of the City 89
　　Friday morning in New York 91
　　September Eleven 93
　　Letter 95
　　Business Crush 97
　　See You Tomorrow 98
　　Walking the Dog in Town 101
　　San Francisco Chronicle 102

Places and Feelings 105
　　California 107
　　Concert in the Woods 108
　　My Dream Dome of Horses 110
　　Morning as an Ordinary Gift 112
　　Domestic Symphony 113
　　How Is Beauty 114
　　Life 115
　　Late Autumn 116

Virus Pandemic.. 117
Haikus of Disquietude..................................... 118
Haikus of Love... 119
Sea of Light.. 120

Postface **121**

Acknowledgments **131**

About the Author **133**

Preface

The Poetry of Lifting Potatoes

To ask a farmer of poetry is a strange request, worse yet a potato farmer. I have known Horia for a long time, to a time before either of us imagined being grandfathers. We were compatriots in what is the durable and subtle empire of the potato. He a researcher, I the actual dirtball. As fellow writers we were a touch odd for our earthy environment, whence came a certain compassion for each other. Of a poet caught, or perhaps trapped, in this hectic, grimy business of agriculture.

As an essayist I'm not well mannered compared to the spare words of the poet. As a story writer I do approach words rather like a Lenco potato harvester comes to the harvest. In bulk form. Lots of words, though I'd never admit to excess. Decent people do not recognize the Lenco reference. In practice a farm machine the size of a nice house, wheels the size of small sheds, propelled by traction motors capable of lifting off the face of the earth every fall to avail the potatoes laying beneath.

A Lenco is not a poetic thing. Monstrosities are not often seen as poetic. This machine hogs the town road. Impatient drivers honk at it. The Lenco disembowels the earth 12 rows at a time. It bellows. It smokes. It smells. It leaks. It works. It isn't poetic.

Poetry is a potato fork. I have several. With a fork you feel the earth, feel gravity, feel the lifting, feel the worms, feel the soil, feel the sweat, feel the tilth. And if you are like Horia and me, feel the godliness of the potato.

This book of poems by Horia is not that monster Lenco, instead a potato fork. Poetry equipped with a short handle to feel the gravity of our lives, its worms, its tilth. A forkful at a time, digging is necessary, and in the lifting, to feel the earth's desire. These words of this potato researcher I'm so honored to know and call friend.

Justin Isherwood

writer and potato farmer,
in Plover Township,
below the moraine where
all the streams run west.

Northwoods Songs

Potato

Eager to grow to catch the light
He sprouts impatient in store's night.

Soon he'll cover this land of ours,
Praising Lord with sea of flowers.

While underneath in room of prayers
He tells the Master his intime cares.

He fills with tubers the soil bed
As Jesus multiplied the loaves of bread.

The labor's fruit is hid in ground
As virtue humble and profound

At dinner baked he opens chest
As Jesus broke the bread and blessed.

Only God Whom all we seek
Could make potato so unique.

Hot Summer Dry Day

Willy-nilly,
another hot summer day.

Waked at first bits of light
over his doghouse,
Spud ran to hunt and play.
He barked with low-key guile
at one end of sprinkler pipes,
lunging for a squirrel catch
at the other end of pile.
He scoured dark,
hidden places in the wood,
sniffing for more knowledge
and a much merrier mood.
But now,
hit by the heat of noon,
under monotonous drone of flies,
thoughts strewn,
he is getting loose,
stretched on grass
in a sparse shade,
in a good snooze.
The silence is piling up.
From the house the far voice
of a self-possessed radio
is saying to itself
important pitted words.
Now and then
touched by a scorching beam

Spud goes to his bowl
for warm, bland water,
too lazy to try striding
to a far creek's hole.

Long days, short warm night,
careless vacation.
Jimmy could stay longer
in the barn to fix his kite.
A bat was whizzing
in the late dusk
veering above his head
in a velvet flight.
Yesterday he hurt the rooster -
a sling unlucky shot.
In bed after supper
Jimmy waked up many a time
crinkling his small pillow
to hear bogeymen's trot
and their scratch at window.
Now it is very boring:
no cousins at home,
no arrowheads
on the old Indian site,
no tree sap gums to chew,
no birds caught in little traps,
no wind to fly the kite.
One feels eternity in the silence
of the ruminating cow.
Once there was a creek
knee-deep and alive…

Now an idle runnel flows instead,
without odd shapes of rocks
on its half-naked bed.
The sun, a tireless fire,
makes the thirst worse.
In grandpa's stable
he'll try to saddle the old horse
and tight the girth a little more.
He'll ride it to the village
for a coke
at Mister Abel's dusty store.
Up high on horse's back
he will not fear passing
by the big corn fields
stretched along the road.
The ceaselessly rustling leaves
sound like a hiding place
from which bad men can jump.
Later, over lunch, he'll stop
for grandma's cranberry cobbler
a relish for everybody's throat.
And who knows,
grandpa might have some
ginger beer ice cream float.

After a deflated, breathless night
and swarms of downy moths
in the mirage of outdoor lamps,
at the early morning crack
Father hurried in his old
and quite rusty pickup truckbig calloused hands on
stirring wheel

bugs smashed against windshield,
to trigger the rain gun
in the very thirsty field.
There is much to do a day:
to till, to spray, to spread the sludge,.
to buck the hay.
Men are wired with steel cables.
The heat is richly flowing
throughout the throttle
deep into his lungs.
Tonight on his way home
after he reached his goal,
he will stop with all his gear
for a strength renewing,
good and very cold Pabst beer.

Lord leads us beside calm waters,
He restores our very soul.

Bryan's Dawn

"What is time?"
the wind inquires
and the tree's many green ears,
shiver, listen, start to wonder
mused by guiles above and under.

Bryan bid farewell to stars
as the fading darkness sailed
through the crispy air
full of sheer expectations.
The chores were waiting
quiet but demanding
a work that never failed.

In the solemn silence
he could hear
coming on its way,
from the giant space,
the frail breath
of a new born day.

A twinkling distant star
was sliding under a bough
stretched across the heights
like a brawny and long arm.

Life is a continuous change.
Deaf and mute

the earth is revolving -
an awkward ballerina,
big and strange.

Anxious stays the farm.
Morning keeps unfurling.

The Two White Ducks

Before going on vacation
our neighbor asked to care,
at the time of season end,
of his snow-white, merry ducks,
two fabulous sisters
he'd like to spare.

A little sleepy, undecided,
to come out of the coop
and enjoy a blessed day,
the dog loved to stir them up
in the brittle morning air,
a crony chasing them
to a boosting rush to play.

Loitering on the grass
to pick the tastiest clover
they spent high quality time
in an unceasing chatter,
with humor, cheerfulness.
sparkling gossip and updates
in all that seemed to matter.

But the most delightful hours
before the sunset's smolder
were at the noon's tame fire,
when they could glide in peace
on the mirror of the pond,
diving for tadpoles and weeds,
 happy, free of any dire.

We lead them evenings to the coop,
waddling back on oboe tune,
swaying through the meadow,
looking like two sailing boats.
The wind gusts chilled the dusk,
to rob the woods of color coats.

Menacing bent tusks of light
cleaved one morning
the woods' thick shadow.
A little brown scat at the gate
blurred the glitter of the dew.
Wasn't the dog of our neighbor.
Onto the humid meadow
we let the ducks get out,
and resumed our daily labor.

The night we were tired
and forgot to lock the gate,
we heard filled with eerie feelings
the wailful choir of the leaves,
the coming brass of winter,
and we knew we're watched.
but we missed their meanings.

At the frigid hours of the dawn
the barn was white of frost.
The gate was wide open,

the door-forced coop deserted
and nothing left beyond.
Feathers, carcass, blood on shore.

An open-wing duck frozen dead
in the silver ice of pond.

The two white buddies knew
the escape was on the water.
The real freedom is from fear
even if might end in death.
Friendship holds the world together -
two bodies in a soul's eternal breath.
The sun is high, the sky is clear.
Over the pond – a flight for ever.

Planting at the Experimental Station

Blinded by the bright white snow
we enter the potato cellar
swallowed
by its devouring darkness
like in a grave.
Perching on the sorter's stand
showing signs of wear,
the friendly glim of a little bulb
welcomes us
with a wink of eye,
in a wave of air.

One by one,
we grab, we heave, we groan,
we lift, untie and dump mesh bags
and freed, oval and round shapes
chase each other,
roll in a happy run
as a gay array
on the sorter's length
to a pensive halt,
innocent victims
at Last Judgment Day
to the breeder's fault.

After a whole winter,
of paper, oakum, spuds,
mice now fall easily trapped
craving for a newer taste.

The snow coat starts to tear
and let our eyes discover
ground squirrels' maze.
Soon, the Canadian geese
will rip the blue sky open
with their military trumpets,
shrill signal over our heads.

Grading, chipping, virus testing,
tuber cutting, run in haste.
Soon, after snow-patched Easter,
the planting ritual time will bless
the soil's cold reviving beds.

The big potato farms' operations
with their romance of large storage bins,
long grading lines, conveyors, trailers,
mighty trucks, and six-row planters,
are far from small-plot planting
as always the stronger, elder brothers.
But both valiant
against-time battles share
and leave the stubborn earth
in a new geometry
of hummock-hills and flair,
like a celestial, outward music,
for a floating hope and prayer…

Harvest

The season is over,
time is ripe and heavy.
Fed by summer's opulence of light
the trees are dressed for feast
in blinding gold and rubies,
and vestments very bright.

The silver mark of frost,
the liquor of the foggy air,
the dark rollers of rain cohorts
fill soul of rush and dare.
The bugles, trumpets, cymbals
call for digging
Now we will see
what we have done.
Meticulously
we'll sift the gain:
the penny-by-penny
deposited by Mother Nature,
the cost of our errors,
the tares and the grain.

If planting was a battle
the harvest is a war.
The smell of dessicant
increases the heat of wait.
The woods are blazed
and mirrored
upside down in heaven's lake.

Soon the army will invade:
tractors, diggers and stone pickers,
harvesters to windrow'rs linked,
trucks with trailers, long conveyers,
bags, crates and wood containers,
all at fast and busy pace.
Within a month
the potato bulky rivers
we have triggered
will quiet down
in a dark,
well-protected place.

The ground is covered
by gold and crimson carpets.
The sun, a giant pumpkin,
is draped in veils of fog,
Birch-tree lines will now hashure
the in-hinge-swinging longer nights.
Somebody above might say:
"Soul take your ease,
the diligence of the green summer
is permanently gone,
it's time for Thanksgiving
and becoming merry.
Your work is deftly done."

First Day

It snowed.
Protractedly.
A white, descending silence,
blanketing people, trees and cars.
Late in the night, the moon
snuck out and froze its light
in shiny blades.

Sipping my hot coffee
and watching the clock
I feel through frosty panes
the janitor bundled-up,
his nerve-scratching blower
freeing the sidewalk.

The first day of my new job
will start in a few hours.

The sun is still sleepy,
the unscented air bites.
I find my way on campus
to Allen Garden house
among rushing students,
faces wrapped in comforters.

In the office, friendly smiles
and a welcoming heat
are smoothing my entrance
into tangled meanders,
unforeseen from the driver's seat.

My superior takes me
to the Student Union stores
like a careful Santa Claus.
Double-insulated boots
fit a spoiled Californian guy
summoned by the polar laws.

Suddenly we hear outside
multipedes and voices.
The door bounces open
in a burst of snow and sun:
my future good friend
and his family are in.
Five Cherubs fill the room
like a blessing spin -
a sage, a narrator,
a crawler, a contemplator,
and a still intra-uterine.
We are now a team
ready for the joy of North,
the land of the man who dares.

As a good-bye to the city
we enter the Capitol Building
stepping up on flights of stairs.
Our glance widens up
to the above giant ring of dome
like water circles after pebbles' kiss.
We cheer Old Abe,
the "Live War-Eagle,"
and the brave fighters
perished in the shadows' bliss.

Now we are ready to drive forth -
friendly waves the Golden Lady,
we are heading North.

The road cuts through the space
a stretched ribbon to a call.
Woods and hills remain behind.
Not for long, sun cuddles all -
gilds silo caps of lonely towers,
slides on humps of gambrel barns,
merry plays in sheets of snow.
We have to hurry
Fleet Farm store's another stop
and it's much more way to go.

We meet Roger,
my next travel mate.
As dusk warns us
with festive red
we load the pickup truck
with doors and windows
for our new dreamed shed.

We navigate
through growing gloom.

Like distant lamplets,
windows glitter -
little hopes across
long alien plains.
The woods around us zoom.

We pass through Parrish,
one-house village,
and here we are:
the Farm,
the nest of goals and battles
as much as we can take.

The starry dome's on watch,
the night is crisp and bold.
The snow in dark is mute with ache:
we are white lambs
branded with the Sign of North.
"Is that the roar of wolves?"
"No, snowmobiles on lake."

We have a job to bloom and hold
our fingers tight on helm.
As said by Aldo Leopold,
creation is for gods
but one can circumvent
all the restrictions
without long wait -
the Potato Realm
we'll reinstate.

Tennis

Wednesday night is tennis time.
No more tractors and work at farm,
no more chores, no more harm.

Competing has specific values
and a peculiar spicy taste.
It's a matter of will and pride.
"Winning isn't everything
but the only thing," Lombardi said.
Sport connects very tight
heart, mind, body, in subtle ways.
It's the country of the Packers
where everybody's a cheesehead.

Thunder serves and fierce returns,
ground strokes gunning,
shots of canny touch and angle,
volley slams and feathered kicks,
drop shots coming by surprise,
fiery minds and secret plans,
line-scorch blistering forehands.
Each shot takes a surface bite.
Running crazy, silk or stony,
balls weave courts
with greenish light.

Outs and nets burn our heart,
"Doubt is being,"
said Descartes.

Two-Four, shut the door,
Four-Five, we are alive -
claws on back dictate the score.
Nobody feels wilted,
nobody huffs and puffs,
we battle like nevermore,
We challenge our fate -
it's no time for life to wait.

Sky slowly melts its golden ends,
with shredded clouds in disarray.
I'll deeply miss my tennis friends
when I'll be home, so far away.

Hodag's Purgatory

I was told
that in a mystical sense
the soul of a cremated lumber ox
needs seven years to cleanse -
one year longer at least
than its exhausting life.
Otherwise,
from his dead ashes
a wild beast might arise -

shooting flames through nostrils,
defending with large horns,
grabbing with sharp claws;
ripping with its fangs
fresh catches in muddy bogs;
chewing with glinting teeth
turtles, snakes, human flesh,
and, Sundays, white bulldogs.

Whimsical, bizarre,
his nervous tail, ever active,
felling trees,
prone he was to cry
sorely, bitterly,
seeing him not attractive
in the Boom Lake's mirror,
lake he made, on a boring day,
dumping cannonballs
in a lonely puddle,
in a reckless play.

Ahh, isn't ugliness
a nature's common feature
and can't it make some wonders
inside a good, fine soul?
Who else ever
put together
oxen's strength,
snake's sagacity,
bear's bravery,
fox's ingenuity,
into a tuneful whole?

Such an uncanny creature,
neither viviparous,
nor mammal, but oviparous,
such an intriguing blend,
neither ichthyosaur nor mylodon -
a missing evolutionary link
that Smithonians think
it's hard to comprehend.

A voice of changing pitch
echoed by the woods
of pine and beech,
an alluring figment
drenched in unknown pigment,
he was named by JFK,
in his speech to nation:
a subject of
"a controversial conversation."

But we know the sinner,
the slave of the temptation,
the ever dreaming teen,

the prankster, the never loser,
the intelligent, humorous Gene
the resourceful timber cruiser.
We know the infamous fellow
bringing fame
to the place of sturdy, driven,
coarsened lumber men,
to the north woods' kingdom
sprinkled everywhere
with a lovely lake,
and the wild beauty
of the Eden break.

The Hodag Bell
from Gene's sternwheeler
coveted in high-school games;
the Hodag blessed
Country Music Festival,
filling souls and air
with sounds and flames;
the smooth back
with shaggy hair
through which winds blow
October's Beer Barrel Polka;
the tail spike
as a real piece of art
and a stick for marshmallow –
all these wear
his candid print of heart.

Over canyons of oblivion
and dark appalling meadows
washed by deluging storms,
sun shouts at prayer's end.

White wings of angels
from blue heights descend
and slide the arch of rainbows.
The soul of the cremated ox
in bygone days beguiled,
cleansed by people's love,
smiles now, clean and dried,
changed and reconciled.

My Love Is Far

The musky catch is very big -
the angler yells overwhelmed.
In nature's tree that's just a sprig.
You are so far and discontent.

The storm has whipped the lake.
I cannot find of you a trace,
The trees watch me with humid arms,
my path to you is lost in maze.

Dark clouds skate down the sky
and oily shadows grab my soul.
 The bridge is slippery, I wonder why,
afraid I am I'll break your bowl.

Your anger flutters through my mind
I have to lure everything
that quiets down my clatt'ry heart,
no matter it might bring.

The coming dark
gives night a pensive start,
the sullen waves are draped in sleep,
the fishes swirl in glossy water.
The bowl is empty -
it's your smile I want to keep.

Deer Day

Finally, the morning came
for the revenge yearned so long.
Eventually the load of discontent
for warped hoods and bumpers
caused by striking on the road,
for butchered fields and gardens,
allowed was to explode.

For fewer days
than fingers on two hands,
the Will may overflow the dam
and the Mind may enjoy
the game of hide and seek.
For the best rack
the Pride and Ego
may now compete.

The thin rind of snow
bites our boots.
It might mark the silent silky tread,
the delicate and fickle moods,
the ever ready wire spring,
the heart-shaped hoofs, the gentle touch,
the eerie whisper of the woods.

But first, let's pause
for a hunters' snack:
in a full of smoke little shack
in a big turmoil,
sizzling pancakes and short brats,

as only men know how to spoil,
while bragging and unveiling
tall tales in little chats.

The sparks of day
draw trails in dark.
The eye starts jogging
through the bushes.
The barrel glitters patiently
accomplice mate.
The claws of waiting
scraping nerves,
are persistent
like a noxious toothache.

Nothing
than the breath of wind,
nothing
than the neutral brush of cold
nothing
left to care,
nothing
seen to spare…

Finally, a shy doe
like a gentle kiss of air…
Another one. No lover yet?
Hush! Remote in the light
flat and gray,
is the fork
of a verdant buck!
Nay.
Probably another day…

My binocular
is glossing the forest.
A flash, a dance, a snort,
then silence.

Is that a heavy branch
behind his head?
Can my will make him turn?
Just a little bit!
His nose is flaring,
the head up
in a pungent watch.
My temples beat.

My manly pride
kicks and burns
without dread.
I flinch, brace, square and pull.
He crumples thunder-stricken.
The sun falls dead...

Soon the delight of dinners
will be over
and the pride forgotten.
What remains is the story
about a beautiful King
in woods and bogs,
a memory sparkling,
and the trophy on the wall
for visitors' dogs
to practice barking.

Winter in Northwoods

At 50 below that winter
I broke by far my own record
with my body spoiled
by the Californian sun.
My home thermometer was too short.
The cheerful flames in the fire place
were not a mere legend
but a warm welcome.

One night a blizzard whipped the ground.
Snow flurries were thrashing the panes.
The wind was raking the forest,
boughs wanted to follow him, spellbound.
Howling in the pipe of chimney
the wind rattled the shed locked door,
and tried to snatch the shuddering
sheet metal roof of the small store.
Mingled with dead's bone sounds,
bugles were unceasingly blown.
Gnashing was the mother nature
in an unending giant moan.

The blizzard went on in the morning
in a blinding swirl of snow
but slowed down at noon,
terribly tired, with no more blow.
A heavy snowfall filled the air
and a pure-white robe, unfurled,
richly covered the stained earth.

A deep silence marked the night
like at the beginning of the world.
Pearled and dim the windows' light.

That very evening full of awe,
the neighbor lady and her daughter
knocked at my friend's door.
In the two-foot drift of snow
they could not find their home key
under the mat as used before.
They and I were offered to sleep
in my friend's family's large nest.
Five children and one on her way
great blessings bring down and keep.
Full of toys was grandma's chest.
French fries filled the oven tray.

I remember the snows of yesteryear
the horse sleds with merry bells,
the caroling for apple, nuts and cheer
when the stars on the high sky spark.
The sleighing from the top of knoll,
the frosty panes, the flowers of thin ice,
the fire flames dancing in the dark.

The childhood part of my old soul
is clean like snow and never dies.

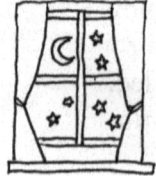

Birds and Seasons

Forgotten are the WINTER's too long nights
when the raven's eggs cracked of cold,
goldfinches burrowed into white snow drifts
chickadees fluffed feathers, alert and bold.
The sun brings color to the growing days,
the skis rustle on the sinuous golf course
and make grouses flush out from under logs.
Shattering the black-and-white loneliness
of the naked trees, sparrows are chirping,
flying tirelessly in their wintry togs.

Large cohorts of geese open the SPRING's gates
with festive honks, with thaw and waterfowl.
Days overfill with bustle, tweeting, flutter.
Nights, sacred calls of loon and hoots of owl.
Dandelions weave their romance in meadows.
Turning home at dusk from tater planting,
a peenting, puffing, mincing dotty woodcock
ends in the car's grille his love dance.
Unseen from a dead irrigation pump
a brooding robin watches as we walk.

SUMMER is the maturity of year.
Flowers giggle dizzy of their own scent,
red-winged blackbirds dine on indian corn,
wrens warble while into the sun ascent.
The light spreads gold on our flapping banner,
undaunted eagles soar with mighty wings.
Gushing, gurgling in the cooled crystal air

at dusk after black storms the thrusher sings.
The goatsuckers, nighthawks, zigzag with flair,
bluebills pitch lakeward for their evening peace.

Gold and ruby is Nature's dress in FALL.
With joyous laugh the leaves bury my feet.
It's cornucopia, harvest feast time,
from red dogwoods in ecstasy robins tweet.
But soon frosts and fogs make a farewell call.
A flowing, scintillating trill's last show -
life is a come and go, idylls don't last.
We watch the cranes fly above the stubble
outran by geese, a cadenced rowing fleet.
All absorbed by a space remote and vast.

Widespread desolation remains behind.
Chilly winds bring mourning rains on their wings,
sodden nights grow, darken the earth and grind.
Lonely circling ravens tower over -
they do not sow or reap, they have no barn.
Silent eternity hides in the heights -
one cannot always doubt the all unseen.
Elusive flocks of birds flutter and yarn.
They snow over our disrobed, black world
for a Christmas, white, peaceful and serene.

Father – Son Poems

Lullaby
5 month-old

Sleep well my baby son,
let a dainty web wrap soon
the tiny creatures of the room.
Sweet dreams, the day is gone.
You are tired, so's the sun.

Gently lay down your head
in your little pillow nest,
the light has lost its crest
with sparkling dancers.
Close your tiny eyes,
another day will come
to find more answers.

See, all shadows sleep,
their weight sinks them deep.
You are free to fly,
you are light and high
my darling angel.
Sleep well my baby son,
the ants of day are gone.

We all hide
a prisoner inside
as an insidious request.
Only love holds the key
of a peaceful rest.

My Little Son and the Geometry
5 year-old

At the spot above
where ceiling stops
the walls start
their white tops.

At the spot where
walls decide to stop
for the first time,
the window starts
its bluish pantomime.

From the sill where
the transparence
gets tired flying,
the walls restart
their story down,
hastily replying.

But in the very spot
where the walls
depart for a second time,
my son's eyes, blue,
start looking too.

With his shy chime
he questions the sky,
rising up on his toes,
perdu.

The Impossible
5 year-old

Would you slide down a snowy mountain with a
                                                                           sled?
Yes, I already did that in our backyard.

Would you ride a wild stallion through fields and
                                                                         woods?
Yes, I already did that on my wooden foal.

Would you drive an off-road truck on steep hill
                                                                           trails?
Yes, I already did that with my toy in the sand box.

Would you fly above the clouds and look down to
                                      the antlike people?
That I don't know.

A man did that, flying like the eagles do.
Who is he? I'd like to meet him and see his shoe.

Domestic Epic
15 years old

Without much notice,
as the ivory foam
creeps on top of waves,
life drags us on the ridge of age.
Our grey haired souls
breathe short on shore,
as ocean splashes
its warning drops of rage.

We gaze at our teenager –
a mountain just emerged
in our yard through foliage.
From now we only may
smooth its sky piercing slopes
with equity from far offstage.

Adventure in our souls
was not consumed by Time
this celestial bastard mage.

Silent Watch
15 years old

Listen,
the horn is calling
the thoughts are rustling.

Look,
through nets of leaves
red flames are hustling.

Forget
the muddy spots
the lure of dark.

Keep
your thoughts unbroken
with a spotless mark.

Hour will come
when you'll learn
the power of the word.

Then my teenage son,
full of fire your thought
will become a sword.

Water Is Soft

Water is soft and humble.
Shapeless, it fills any vessel.
Its steadiness solves the rock,
its run carves the stone.

I miss my grandpa
his gentle smile, his faith,
his calloused hands and legs,
his benign tone.

Life of the Poems

Every Story

Every story has a pair of shoes
of special brand
that wanders
stepping on dust, clay or sand,
hesitating on broken glass,
engraving in mud or snow
in a slight utter,
or with high class
and gentle touch
walking on the water…

The Birth of the Word

There is a thin
unseen threshold
between the thought
and the word
that carries it through.

It's sunk in a dense
and cut-off shadow.

Teach me my Lord
to use the cue to master
from head to tip-toe
the new-born word.

My Poem

My poem sheds badly.
It spreads words all over the place
including soft and clean carpets.
It scatters translucent metaphors
in street intersections at semaphores.

People tried to vacuum them
but their tools stalled clogged.
When they cleaned the bags
they found dense blue strips
tied in many tiny knots.

They did not know
that these were my ineffable,
sky-born thoughts
that coagulate entangled,
hardly visible and silent,
when mishandled.

Beauty
is an interrupted dream.

Of Course

Of course,
there are also inventors
of chemicals
that catch everything
in their net of odors.
The commercials say
you have just to spray
and then to wipe thoroughly.

It doesn't work with words.
The shadows of all poems
escape unobserved
under the ceiling
and if you look up carefully
you can see them gleaming.

At the family supper time
they drop like dew
in the salad dressing
while lightly they touch hearts
with a noiseless blessing.

The Poem Punctuation

The shut-up
or the wise, relaxing end
imposed by the period,
the comma's submissive bend
or the uncontrolled pant
when there are so many things
to be said about,
the colon's call
for patient listening
others' voice's sheen,
the compromise begged
by undecided semicolons -
all are bumbling
on the computer screen
for a flavored story flume,
sliding on the slant of light
that sagely crosses
the air of my upper room.

The poem's scaffold
arduously grows
step by step.
Blessed sevenfold,
the poem ends all wired
with a net of nerves.

Then it reacts
unpredictably,
and as a living being
it eagerly imparts.
Its love spreads
and richly floods
the rooms of hearts.

Spring Day

Honey and water
shine in the air
after rain.
Fully pitted
light words flutter
down the drain.

I squelch through mud
its tiny flowing string,
the unbraiding colors
from the hidden sun,
as a love duet
over a golden ring.

A chain,
of lust and sweat,
chants in the mid of day.
O, darling,
my so-far-away darling,
what more
can I say?

The Poem's Fate

Always the poem
precedes the word.

Sometimes it waits for us
to come with the last lines
like an impatient airplane
seeking a lane to land
and enjoy the world.

But the most time
we leave it inside
for the combustion
of the heart,
without ever
dressing it in words
and letting it
to come out
for a flight
into the day light.

The Song of Heart

The poem is a dream
that floats regular things
on waters of unknown
among the transparent
lilies of the heart.

Sometimes the words are late
and the long-waiting,
immaculate paper
is silent like the hour
when a stunt pilot dies
and the heart is stabbed.

Then,
like a cue stick
knocking pool balls
a sword spreads
colored words
and they flood the large, white space.
Heart enlightens meadows,
Mind stretches highways.

The canvas of the poem
is now
unfolded under your feet.
Be careful
my love,
when you walk on it.

Thy Love, O Lord

Psalm 1

Without You Lord
my life journey
became
a dirty hostile wall
full of graffiti,
a wall with a hole
made for a corridor
dark and alien.
If I rove through,
stepping on years,
tiny gnats
oily spiders
silty rats
venomous snakes
waylay me
and feed my fears.

Fortunately
I still have
Your light
and my prayer's
shaky ladder
to lead me out
of pitch
dark layers.

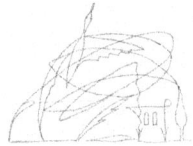

Psalm 2

Lord, here's again the soft temptation
as a cruel feline for its raw meat
to tear up the peace of heart
to shove me wounded in the street.

Lord, please draw my shaky soul
from the night's cold and sticky dough,
pass her over the scary, giddy void
and raise her above the stormy flow.

If You'll nest her into stone
a spring blessed by Your breath will roam.
If You'll carve her into wood
she'll play Your name in a gracious mood.
If You'll sew her in a carnal dress
Your glory in humans she will then express.

Psalm 3

Life is a ruthless grinder.
My body became a soiled
worn out dress.
Its rags have polished
my stony soul
strapped in trials,
snares and stress.

Lord, you share my yoke,
the sorrow's vivid fire
the toilsome road,
the painful loss.
Loaded with tears
I fall in the abyss
of Thy holy cross.

A viscid water freezes
my arms and I am trapped
in large whirlpool rings.
But Thy loving care
lifts quietly my body
and gives my soul
white sturdy wings.

Psalm 4

Speak to me my Lord
tell me about Thee
when I go again astray,
and be the ripe Noon,
the summit of the Light
and the power of the Day.

I have enough hearing my voice
in my prayers strapped.
Fill me with the will of Thine,
see how selfish I am wrapped.
Chill me with Thy river stones,
with Thy tears of love on cross
with Thy large unknowns.

I'm on the shore, my Lord,
of Thy endless power's ocean.
For the sake of our Feasts,
Thou squeezed the heavens' world
and Thy vast celestial coat
on a flat and narrow wooden cross,
and on the humble hairy back
of a never ridden colt.

My soul is like an open wound
weaving clumps of blood.
I call Our Lady's holy icon
who looks at Holy Infant's face
blessed with gold-light flood.

His wise, heavy-of-age eyes
are filled with love and grace.

The fragrance Lord
that Thou have sent
is strong but light
like the glittery dew of mornings,
like the subtle scent
of the vestments of the sunsets.
It is mint, basil and myrrh
brought by magi guided
by forgotten, vagrant planets.

Here down I feel the knife
of my affirming tomb.
Look Lord I'm here,
tightly draped in gloom,
with Thou I come to life!

Psalm 5

O Lord hearken to my voice.
It's madness in the valley
the cup of sorrow overflows.
Sickness blanket chokes the earth
the day is swallowed by the night
be next to me, be ever close.

My soul starves for Holy Bread.
You said at Jacob's well
that You have thirst.
I know you walk amidst all these.
Give me Your eyes and ears,
teach me what comes first.

Help me the burden to unload,
it's time of scrutiny and sieve.
Light please my long waved road
I drag my feet, I need big wings,
I know Love patiently waits
I have to learn how to receive.

Psalm 6

So often I cannot see Thou Lord,
so often I am down, defeated.
Revive please the pure child
out of my deep inmost being.
Make me to cry relieved
like the healed Bartimaeus.
Give me back to life
as perfect as you fashioned me
from the very beginning.

To You light and darkness are alike
and a bright day is the night.
"Walk the good trail,"
the blind was told,
"Faith restored you fully."
and at once his eyes caught sight
clear and bold,
exploring on its own,
and anointed with love
he wanted to follow You
in the limitless unknown.

O, Lord, be kind,
give me agile thought,
unwavering step
bestow upon my walk,
bring me to fullness
as you healed the blind
and redirect my way

to enter and to not miss
the blessed silent cloud
and gladsome light
of the resplendent sunset
of an accomplished day
and of Thy wholesome promise.

Thorns of Intrusion

Make Thou O Lord
the intruder myrrh and joy
and not a wielding sword.
Let his charge with filthy boots
show Thine spotless face
as in orchards apples shine
from Thine Holy Light a trace.

Give me not O Lord
the stab of shrill impatience
nor the selfish thirst of salt.
But leave the soul feel fault
and make the comer
the mellow breeze
of a Holy Summer.

Keep me in Thy breath
if it is the kiss of death.

Autumn Dusk

Do you hear
horn calls, far in the woods?
Countless thoughts are rustling.

See,
through moving shadows
delusive flames are tussling.

Look,
the copper leaves of trees
ignite pockets in the air.

Watch
the birds' mysterious move
with all splendor they can wear.

Forget
the many staining spots,
the meanings of the dark.

Leave
thoughts unbroken
with a spotless mark.

The Hour will come
when they'll sever
the whites of Life.

With land
they will split
oceans like a knife.

Then,
they will flow
with slow warm breath

far,
beyond
the murky Death.

Anxious Hour

The air shimmers
in a deceiving wind.
The corn field
is full of whispers
like a haunted place.
The compact canopy
of the potato field
shudders, shudders
in a continuous sigh.
Don't be afraid.
Don't crouch down,
crushed by complaints
and questions "Why,"
Let's sit on porch
and talk.

See, the poplars shush us.
Don't speak too loud -
you'll wake up the passions
that will start to boil
our old and tired hearts
worn by long years
of scorn, arthritis,
and never ending toil.
Look up and come in sight
of the eternity touch
that hides blessings
on slants of light
in the wrinkles of the sky.

Ignore the mobs of thoughts
that ceaseless bounce and bob.
Don't let your soul to coil
in despair, washed by tear.
Far are candid woods
splashed with silence
and caressed by fog,
the life surrounds us here
with its infinite care,
the Hands of Lord.

Let's sit on porch and talk
and learn to spell
a wholesome word:
Agape.

Poems of the City

Friday morning in New York

The city anoints itself
with gray oily dawns.
The streets stretch
their legs numbed
on dreamed lawns.
The subway starts
its worried flight
to peck and spare
the last grains of dark
in Time Square.
Half-asleep
long snakes of cars
themselves uncoil
and suddenly excited
the crowds of sounds
begin to call each other
in an endless big turmoil.
I know they'll pierce the light
all the day long
with their yell, whisper,
shout, groan and song,
tenacious and mean
taxing my patience
and my zeal of work
fed with caffeine.
So many things
can't be done
at a drop of hat!

I'll be entangled
in numerous duties,
before this Friday
will die as all
the beasts and beauties.

Tomorrow I will be
far from fierce
cohorts of sounds.
I'll fish upstream on Hudson
forgetting all my bounds.
And while I'll watch
the velvet fish
quietly sliding by,
white croups of clouds
will silently trot
on the trails of sky.

September Eleven

News was like
drinking air, eating bullets –
The first was unbelievable,
the latter made the heart
to bleed forever.

With metal taste
infamous blasts,
under the limpid eyes
of the unshakable
Liberty Lady
who lasts.

No need for minds to guess
their final minutes
in perishing planes and buildings.
They became part of us
in their courage, in our sadness
under heaven's ceilings.

And then
it was the sacrifice for others
in the maze of bones of dust:
the painful but fruitful investment
over the sorrow –
life for life
sky for sky
light for light,
the hope of tomorrow.

I know a place
where now
the wind in piety whispers
day and night
his colorless shadows
of distress and grief
preceding
the reviving light.

Letter

From the lighthouse
my yearnings are stripped
blown by winds
like autumn leaves.
The North brings frost and fears,
the South brings stomach fevers.

Not a single needle
could fit amidst the crowd
in the town square.
The strike is boiling,
the worries roar
and erupt
from the body's hips
through the raging mouth.

The prison bus
sharpens its shadow's blade
on the edge of street.
The black top
sweats with blood.
Black spots rise and cry
on the radar screen.

I am sending you
the width of my shoulders,
the rim of my burning heart,
and the shadow of my thoughts,

from the very core of my home.
I'm sending them with love
toward you as far as I can,
I don't know how long they will roam
with their wild and ardent innings.

We are the Quantity's slaves.
The earth has no ends,
the heavens no beginnings.

Business Crush

It's like
the windows liquefied in the air,
the doors escaped from the hinges
which made them daily nod,
the stairs continued their flight
interrupted for some time.
The curtains – arms of wind,
and the lamps with their glaring eyes
were blown in a huge sigh.
The house,
my dream house,
vanished in the crowds of street!

And you wonder why
we cannot meet
though I have some penny left
for "fish and fry"?

See You Tomorrow

It's hard to see you leave.
See you tomorrow!
The streets slice the night,
the dense dark quivers
with whispers and sorrow.

Your tall house
eagerly calls you,
peers at me
with her gothic windows.
On the top of the staircase
reigns implacable
the massive Door
with the draw force
of an imploding star,
self-possessed,
without heart sore.

Not for long
I could you borrow.
Loneliness threatens me
with its long miles…
But, suddenly,
the street lights
tickle Door's wooden fibers
and she faintly smiles.

See you then tomorrow!

Walking the Dog in Town

I like the streets downtown my city –
they have so clear stories to be told
by their lawns, house shapes, and people,
yet I never saw in them a secret world.

I only knew the odor of the garbage cans
shown up at curb at the collection time,
the French fries' whiff from Burger King,
the smell of flatulent cars' mufflers' prime.

Until a dog taught me on a rather sunny day
that every square inch has a mysterious life
and it has to be sniffed, judged and replied
with a spurt in a straight and honest way.

San Francisco Chronicle

I like to keep up with the news,
not from volatile screens
but from solid paper sheet.
Mornings I count my quarters
and buy the newspaper
two blocks from my street.
I even cut the hottest articles
and file them for one year
until they lose their heat.

One day I got the exciting news
I wanted to comment
at our business meeting,
and I hurried up to work
as I knew the time was fleeting.

But I could not leave the place -
the greedy door
of the newspaper box
shut down and grabbed
the end of my tie
defending its own space.

I pulled the handle,
I shook the box,
I banged the door.
I tried to crack it open
with my nail clipper.
I checked if it slides.

But the stubborn spring
did not take sides.

In vain I sought
for other quarters.
In vain I looked for help -
no one was passing by.

So, with a deep sigh,
I called myself a dork,
I untied my beautiful tie,
thinking of the windfall
of the next paper buyer
and I rushed to work.

Since then a bow tie
is what I wear.
With the newspaper
its pattern makes a pair.

Places and Feelings

California

On my forehead's furrows
a sunbeam softly lies.
Naked fairies twirl
and hurt themselves
in the blades of my eyes.
Of too much scorching blue
nobody's left in the skies.

My voice winds
as a snake through my throat.
All around is hot.
Feeling lonely in the air
my pulse is a wrinkled toad.
A dry blood trace
stains the dusty road.

Lord, feed my sweat to reach
a manger - shady and cold,
for I have to nurse
my Time as long as it is still
strong, tense and bold
and not soft and mummified
before becoming old.

Concert in the Woods

The pianist -
a bantam grandma
with knots and snags.
The conductor -
frivolous grandpa
with hair long and sleek.
The teen orchestra -
clean, obedient leaven,
raking dehydrated chords,
and glimmering Mozart -
a playful, joyful creek.

I wonder if the sunset
is still trapped
in forks of roads
and forest breaks,
if the sleeping beauty
is a green enameled glade
mirrored by raptured lakes.

If I might keep pace
with time's race in my veins
and cool my scorched forehead
in the snowy peaks of earth,
my toil would bear fruits of sense -
a scenic river
would wind in universe...

The sweet grandma
is glimmering
among the woody knots,
the branches look bright
through the moisture blots
and I think,
I think I might...

My Dream Dome of Horses

For my foundation
I used a *stallion,*
rented from my neighbor
for wilder rides.
I'll hear his stifled hoof-taps
in my lonely nights.

I fished from my lawn
and carefully glued
on one plastic sheet or more
the dew *horse* of the dawn
to hide my garden door.

I'll turn around a gentle *mare*
when I'll leave
to face the sun
and I'll feel so good
to pass through,
in a horsey mood!

But the fresh scent
of chewed, grazed grass
torments my blinking eyes,
while my *Shetland*'s back
spasmodically jerks
annoyed and stung by flies.

I long to use my trotting Word
and my dream *horses,*
to build my intime
poem and Dome.
But now the earth is sick
covered by self-inflicted wounds,
rabies rage and foam.

Morning as an Ordinary Gift

The skunk arrives each morning with the sun.
Phlox, tango hyssop, Russian sage, black-eyed
                                                    Susan,
Nothing would have surprised him a century ago.

Piles of stone saved from an old foundation
to bring the grade of land up four more feet.
It feels very much like coming home and go.

Beneath the kitchen's window a deep trench.
He fell in love with his big working project.
She'll cook a good dinner for him tonight.

Cash for clunkers, coupons, various cards,
The mailman filled the box up to the brink.
It is strenuous work to do much and right.

We should declutter life, simplify and remain cool.
Empty returns the yellow bus from school.

Domestic Symphony

From the tower
of the Hour
my ears watch
sounds creeping
through the house -

the snore of the refrigerator,
the whistle of the sink,
the squeak of the door,
the sigh of the cabinet,
the whisper of the toilet,
the crack of the wooden floor;

and I try to catch
the hard to hear
the sound of minuet
of the soft ovals
of your moving
silhouette.

How Is Beauty

Like a gentle river,
like a smooth canoe,
like a leaf short shiver,
delicate and graceful
like you.

As a flying kite,
as a stripe of silver,
as a pool of light,
flaming and silky
as dew.

Like a serpent hiss,
like a flower whisper,
like a hallowed bliss,
white and pure
like winter.

As a wit of humor,
as a crazy hue,
as an innocent bloomer,
a versatile genius.
I like you.

Life

Sow a star in your garden,
make moon and lantern look alike
spread a cloud of fire flies,
when you take an evening hike.

Stretch a rainbow to your roof,
cut a stripe of clear sky,
stick a sun kiss on the window,
make another morning try.

Life is an unceasing journey.
with dark and sunny stays.
Night and day the river's flowing.

Earth? A tiny, fragile place.

Late Autumn

The birds are busy
with their journey.
The sun is now tired
And we'll lose it
in the oil pan of earth.
The storms are now
spayed or neutered.

The wise man
bitterly knows:
the symphony,
the richness,
and the gold
precede the uncolored
careless cold,
the truth in black-and-white,
and the bottomless
loneliness.

Virus Pandemic

They gave him a Crown
as to a despotic King
reigning over creeping
unseen twisted fogs.
Hordes of whimsical voids,
fondling, alluring, muffling,
disembodying heart and breath.
Valkiries wait in secret covert
to blast the victim's body
and unfold the shrouds of death.

Their vibe and ambience
chill our endangered bones.
They are around
we don't know where.
We know they're lurking
with tiny steps of silk
adjusted to a furtive clock.
Whose turn will come?
What door they'll knock?

I'm talking now
to you my love.
It's peace.
But they might sail
through me in silence
into a subtle breeze,
with their covert calls
for sinking us in Infinite
which never fail.

Haikus of Disquietude

Maggots crawl away
like spicy thoughts sneaking out.
Butterflies above.

Hearts on a treadmill.
Flapping shadows around us -
whistling wings of dove.

The wind is strapped tight.
In the void of the bridge arch -
sunset's golden knife.

One has paid for us.
On shoulders of strange masters,
what are we for life?

Haikus of Love

Sweet scent from afar.
The wind carries large spaces,
a soft touch of God.

Shapes and all unformed
intone a soundless song.
Clear heights are awed.

Cuddled by soft light
souls slide into each other.
Quiet hours wait.

Never ending joy.
Two in one, on wings of dove,
our love's feather weight.

Sea of Light

Life is the light
hunted by the shadows of death;
they elongate in the dusk of our age
and hide in the thicket of the breath.

A sea inside us
rolls our soul round like stones.
The wind moans
rippling light with darkness.
The sea pounds its waves
upon our glossy bones.

A harbor patiently waits
for our tired soul's frigates
at the sea's unknown end.
There, overloaded with treasures
of dreams, wins and defeats
forced are they the way to wend.

Who will firmly say
how our painful strive
should, could or might be?

The answer waits on quay.

Postface

Yes, Wisconsin is the American Dairyland and a country of corn, potato, cranberry, and ginseng. I never wore a cheesehead hat because, coming from California, I remained a faithful 49er but I loved the place and I made many friends among the Packers' fans. However, first thing that comes in my mind when I think of my dear Northwoods is a triad: bluegrass, tornadoes, and Northern Lights.

Certainly no kind of grass of a weird blue color grows in the prairies or meadows, although such a name was picked up by the local people for a species of Poa. It is the bluegrass music, a kind of music that you hear everywhere willy-nilly. It stirs the young age with romance calls and it sickens the old age with nostalgic memories. It covers a large area of songs with a special sort of longing, melancholy and discontent, from the songs of love, jail or marijuana to those of positive action or religious motivation. As the Saturday mornings at the Rhinelander radio station are dedicated to polkas (ah, I love the three-day Octoberfest!), the Sunday afternoons are dedicated to bluegrass music. A special event in Northwoods is the Annual Hodag Country Music Festival in open air whose sound can be heard many miles far away.

And in addition to all these let us not forget the natural great singers that, as the famous John Muir said, "sweeten Wisconsin." They are the birds. Among them, the brown thrush or thrasher is the champion. Its magnificent singing glorifies the "rosy-purple evenings after thunder showers." Aldo Leopold, a notorious Wisconsinite biologist and meticulous observer, analyzing the goose flocks' flight formula, a multiple of number six, wrote, "It is not often that cold-*potato* mathematics confirms the sentimental promptings of the bird-lovers." I tried to dedicate a poem to the local feathered picturesque world.

The land of the Mid West is in the northern half of the corridor between the warm, tub water like, Gulf of Mexico, and the glacially cold Great Lakes. When they rebel, the warm air masses of the South swoop over the land and ram their heads into the heads of the air powers of the North. The winner earns the supreme right to brush the plains, hills, woods, lakes and houses. Thus, behind the noisy storms with scary lightning that tears the sky dome and hits the earth in anger like a giant stagger, late-afternoon dark tornadoes unfold their insane dance crumbling houses, flipping trees over and flying cars up. The Great Lakes have their own cemeteries of ships sunk by storms. Especially the Superior,

Michigan and Huron Lakes are so huge that the clouds coming from Canada get exhausted before succeeding to cross them entirely and in a big relief decide to immediately unload the huge amount of snow that was intended to bless the fields of South.

These are the big snowdrifts one has to shovel from November to April, besides the annoying persistence of the cold that freezes the car engines and forces everybody to plug in the engine-block electric heater. For a Californian like me, experiencing a night of 50 below was a total thrill. Enchanting white surface, the snow welcomes with joy the arctic breeze that clears the sky and brings the stars to a blinding brightness.

Here, in March 1997, I told good night more than a week to Hale-Bopp, a comet of a ravishing beauty. However, the most memorable moments were the Aurora Borealis watching. As soon as the weatherman on the TV local news at 10 p.m. told us in a confidential tone about its ephemeral presence, I got out that very instant. The sky was covered by delicate veils of pale purple, blue or green light, shimmering in a profound silence. It seemed like a mysterious universe was whispering to us from beyond our terrestrial world.

All these – the bluegrass, the tornadoes which chases you away to the basement, and the Northern Lights, together with the singular beauty of the nature and the harsh climate, create a unique philosophy in the local people. They have a deep understanding of life, a mind of firm certitudes, a warm heart fed by a family of three to five children, a special sense of humor that relishes the long stories with a slow release of the point (not because they are unable to get it right away but because they want to taste it longer), a solid discipline of work and a high respect for the holy things. How could I forget the long winter nights when parents, friends and children gather at the fire place for talking heart-to-heart, while contemplating the play of the warm yellow-reddish flames?

Wisconsin is a place with people keeping in their heart a subconscious nostalgic love for the North, probably because the ancestors of many of them have come from Northern countries. I have a friend who at 18 year age, after finishing the high school, lived a couple of months on a fishing boat in Alaska, in order to prove himself. It is a place where, at every large family reunion, the older generation recites for the others' great delight the very popular poem "The Cremation of Sam McGee" written by "the Bard of Yukon" Robert W. Service which tells the story of a Klondike Gold Rusher.

And in the end, let us not forget that, out of the fifty states of our big country, Wisconsin is on the third place in producing the potatoes that we have on our supper table. My friend Justin Isherwood, residing South of Plover, who is a fabulous farmer writer and harmoniously "combines the material facts of dirt farming with the transcendentalist musings of philosophy" as accurately noted the historian Dave Engel, mentioned some peculiarities of this unique plant. He wrote, "Taters tend to burrow. They're half Irish and predisposed to felonious behavior: sneaking, conniving, avoiding daylight" (*Origin of the Potato Digger* in *Book of Plough*, Lost River Press, Inc., Boulder Junction, Wisconsin, 1996).

I would like to add a few more words about this round-oval fruit of earth - this mysterious character who was my companion during my entire life and to whom I dedicated my dreams and efforts. As our eight-year-old grandson says, "Grandpa is *a potatologist.*" Potato is a special creature. He knows philosophy. He knows that we come from dust and into the dust we return. He likes to study everything in depth. That is why his vines investigate the sun light under the blue sky and their philosophical wonder leads to accomplishments in the depth of the ground. He is a modest being and not a braggart one; in order to learn his talents we must dig. He is wise. He displays with generosity the splendor of a canopy in blossom during the summer but, being aware that everything is transient, he stores carefully his goods in a protected place. He loves his homeland and remains deeply attached to his mother's soil.

I heard from Father Joseph Mary Wolfe a prayer for farmers and I like it. "Creator of Heaven and earth, we praise You, for the goodness of Your creation reveals something of You, the Source of all goodness! We ask You to bless those who farm and make their living off the land. They know of their dependence upon You and look to you to make their crops and livestock fertile and fruitful. Bless them, Lord, with strong faith, healthy bodies, generous hearts and abundance for good works."

The first cycle of poems was inspired by my nine years spent in Wisconsin. Therefore I dedicate this book to the great souls of the people that I was blessed to meet there. They became a luminous part of my life. All of them, not only the matchless potato folks!

However, there are other poems in this book. With few exceptions they deal with major themes of life or reveal deeper meanings from the ordinary day routine. I think poetry should accompany us always in our small or big events, and in our perception of life, because it has the power to enrich our mind and heart. . It is true that poetry requires a more attentive reading and for fully perceiving its complete message we have to spend longer time on a poem of one-two pages than on a ten-page regular story but we need poetry. Poetry can define better our feelings beyond their appearances, it can help us to explore the domains of intuition beyond those of the reason, and it describes better our less obvious relationship with the beings and things around us. It helps us to notice the uniqueness of the thinnest interstices of our busy day agenda and to value their precious weight.

None of the other kinds of writing is able to communicate the ineffable, the difficult to express, that we feel that exists behind the concrete reality of our action. As the great poet Wallace Stevens said in *Opus Posthumous,* "The poet is the priest of the invisible." By its suggestions and metaphors the poetry can makes us to discover all of a sudden something hidden. It is like walking in a very dark stormy night and, at once, the lightning enables us to see for a few moments what is around. Or like the soldiers waiting in trenches in a dark menacing night when a flare throws light for a couple of seconds above the position of the enemy. Or, as another great poet, Carl Sandburg, said about poetry, it is like an opening and closing of a door for a few instants, allowing us to guess what is inside.

It happens sometimes that the phantasy jumps in and the result is a sparkling game of words, like fireworks, water music or a show of kites, for the most delight of our mind. Several poems in this book talk a little bit about writing itself, about the battle with the words for finding the most powerful ones. Didn't Mark Twain said, "The difference between the almost right word and the right word… is the difference between the lightning bug and the lightning?"

The prodigious poet, editor, teacher, essayist, novelist, and playwright Paul Engle wrote in a newspaper article, "Poetry is ordinary language raised to the Nth power. Poetry is boned with ideas, nerved and blooded with emotions, all held together by the delicate, tough skin of words" (in New York Times, 17 Feb. 1957). Therefore we might agree with the famous conclusion of the classic English philosopher Francis Bacon included in his Of Studies, which makes also a reference to poetry lovers, "Histories make men wise; poets, witty; the mathematics, subtle; natural philosophy, deep; moral, grave; logic and rhetoric, able to contend."

Cheers.

Horia Ion Groza

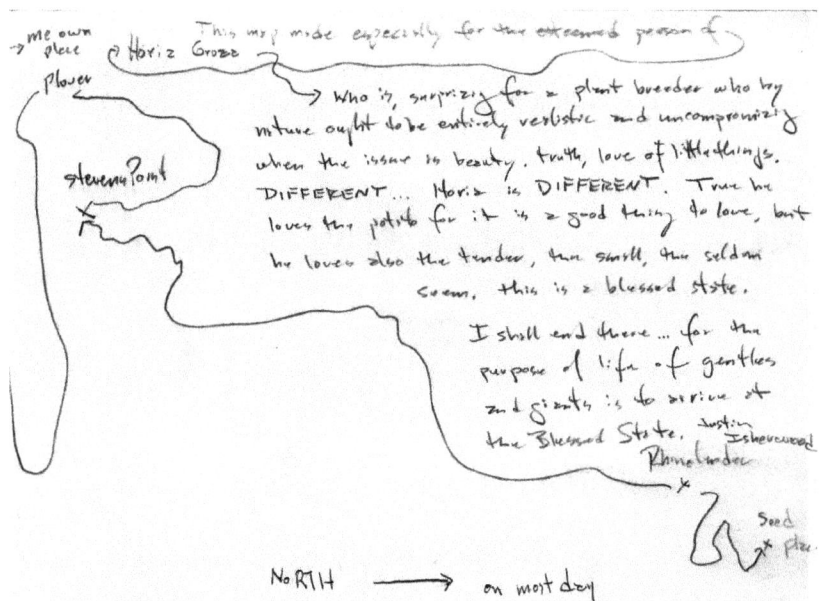

Autograph written by Justin Isherwood for Horia Ion Groza on the first page of his book, *Justin Isherwood, Book of Plough, Essays on the Virtue of Farm, Family & Rural Life* (Lost River Press, Inc. Boulder Junction, Wisconsin, 1996). The road on the map starts from "Seed Place", goes through Rhinelander, Stevens Point, Plover and ends at "my own place:"

"This map made especially for the esteemed person of Horia Groza who is surprising for a plant breeder who by nature ought to be entirely realistic and uncompromising when the issue is beauty, truth, love of little things. DIFFERENT... Horia is DIFFERENT. True, he loves the potato for it is a good thing to love, but he loves also the tender, the small, the seldom seen. This is a blessed state. I shall end there... for the purpose of life of gentles and giants is to arrive at the Blessed State." Sgd. Justin Isherwood.

Acknowledgments

I wish to thank Justin Isherwood and Bryan Bowen for their words of support in this project, and Philip Dunigan who at my retirement party, knowing my future plans, enriched me with an expensive printer and a triad of books vital for my writing. I am very grateful to five highly respected potato specialists: late Joe Pavek and Bob Johansen, my professional breeding mentors on the American land, Tanasie Gorea, late Titus Catelly, and J.T.H. Hermsen, my genetics and breeding mentors in Europe. I would also like to thank the Romanian architect and very talented artist Bogdan Zaharescu, whose three drawings and one painting, made during his visits in United States, embellish this book; the Californian writer Daniel Hallford for all our fruitful discussions; and my family and friends for their continuous love and encouragement.

About the Author

The essayist, poet and novel writer Horia Ion Groza (born in Romania and established in USA in 1986), has a PhD in plant genetics and breeding. He worked 40 years in this scientific research domain for potato crop: 20 years in Romania in a potato research institute, and other 20 years in United States with several bioengineering companies and at the University of Wisconsin-Madison. He authored three books of essays on philosophical and social themes, three books on Christian faith and tradition, two volumes of poems, one novel and one book of literature critique. All of them have been published in Romanian and were received very well by the public. He was rewarded with the LiterArt XXI Prize for journalism (1999) and for essays (2002). Besides this poetry book, he wrote in English language three books on Christian faith which were published in 2016, 2018, and 2019, respectively.

Reflection Books
Books Published by Horia Ion Groza

Discovering the Sacred Time of Our Life

Paperback: 338 pages
Publisher: Reflection Publishing (August 29, 2016)
Language: English
ISBN-10: 1936629461
ISBN-13: 978-1936629466
Product Dimensions: 5.8 x 0.7 x 8.3 inches
Buy on Amazon, Barnes and Noble: $16.98

Living the Sacred Time of Our Life

Paperback: 452 pages
Publisher: Reflection Publishing (February 25, 2018)
Language: English
ISBN-10: 1936629518
ISBN-13: 978-1936629510
Dimensions: 5.8 x 0.9 x 8.3 inches
Buy on Amazon, Barnes and Noble: $18.95

Saint Paisius Velichkovsky of Neamts and Paisianism

Paperback: 230 pages
Publisher: Reflection Publishing (February 28, 2019)
Language: English
ISBN-10: 1936629526
ISBN-13: 978-1936629527
Product Dimensions: 5.2 x 0.5 x 8 inches
Buy on Amazon, Barnes and Noble: $14.98

Viata Maicii Domnului

Paperback: 100 pages
Publisher: Reflection Publishing (June 1, 2011)
Language: Romanian
ISBN-10: 0979761840
ISBN-13: 978-0979761843
Product Dimensions: 6 x 0.2 x 9 inches
Buy on Amazon, Barnes and Noble: $11.95

Reflection Books
Po Box 1413
Citrus Heights, CA 95611-1413